AN ASCENDANCY
OF THE HEART

ROBERT O'DRISCOLL

An Ascendancy of the Heart

Ferguson
and the Beginnings of
Modern Irish Literature
in English

WITH AN INTRODUCTION BY
MÁIRE CRUISE O'BRIEN

MACMILLAN OF CANADA
MACLEAN-HUNTER PRESS

Set in Pilgrim type with Times Roman display
and printed and bound in the Republic of Ireland
at the Dolmen Press
for
The Macmillan Company of Canada
70 Bond Street
Toronto M5B 1X3

ISBN 0 7705 1474 X

For my mother and father,
Newfoundlanders,
who made it possible for me
to spend some years in search
of our Celtic heritage

I am deeply grateful to Professor Lorna Reynolds, Head of the Department of Modern English at University College Galway, without whose constant encouragement and help this monograph would not have been written. I acknowledge too the help with the originals given me by my wife, Treasa, and her sensitive rendering, both in public and private, of the original airs.

I am also grateful to the Canada Council for providing the financial support necessary for the preparation of the monograph.

INTRODUCTION

When the distinguished author of this monograph, my friend Bob, did me the honour of asking me to introduce his work — an honour which I accepted with an enthusiasm which increased as I read — I remembered the following incident. Some time ago, at a reading of poetry in Irish, I heard an impassioned young woman declare that the most truly arresting examples of contemporary Irish verse published recently were to be found in a collection of nursery rhymes issued by the Government Publications Office! She proceeded, with feeling, to recite:

> Rachaidh mise,
> Is rachaidh tusa,
> Siar sa ghleann.
>   Goidfidh mise,
>   Is goidfidh tusa,
>   Mart breá ramhar.
> Crochfar mise,
> Is crochfar tusa,
> Is cad a dhéanfaidh ár gclann?
>   Is cuma leatsa,
>   Is cuma liomsa,
>   Nuair nach mbeimid ann!

In translation this would read:

> I will go,
> And you will go,
> West in the glen.
> I will steal,
> And you will steal,
> A fine fat beast.
> I will be hanged,
> And you will be hanged,

What will our children do?
I don't care,
And you don't care,
Since we won't be there !

At once I experienced a stab of illumination : for here surely was the original of the lines quoted by Dr. O'Driscoll on page 46 as being the earliest known example of verse translated from the Irish language into English.

You and I will go to Finegall.
You and I will eat such meats as we find there.
You and I will steal such beef as we find fat.
I shall be hanged and you shall be hanged.
What shall our children do?
When teeth do grow unto themselves
Let them go to the glens.
(As their fathers did before.)

As so often happens it was a Eureka which had occurred to others before. I had always assumed — and thought myself in good company in so doing — that the English was a translation, satirically literal to the point of parody, of a piece of classical Bardic verse celebrating the cattle-rieving exploits of some Gaelic chief and probably part of a much longer poem in the appropriate convention. Now while I thought over how to approach my present task I had the good sense to check. A friendly response to my first inquiry led me to an article by the late Gerard Murphy in Volume 7 of *Eigse* (1953-55), pages 117-120, entitled 'A Folksong Traceable to Elizabethan Times'. Professor Murphy has set out there, with characteristic insight and scholarship, the fascinating and romantic discovery that we are not here dealing with a praise poem of the type so much reprobated and to be reprobated by succeeding English administrations as conducing to rapine and plunder, but with an actual rievers' ballad — equally equivocal morally, no doubt — sung by the rank and file of the rievers in an Irish indistinguishable from the living speech of our own day and in a metrical form so straightforward and basic as to be suitable to any modern Irish-speaking infant play group! Sitting by the fireside of the famous West Cork folk-scholar and antiquarian Domhnall Bán O Céileachair, Professor Murphy had the surely astonishing experience of hearing from the lips of his host, not only the words of the wicked old song — now the accompaniment of a children's game of the Nuts-In-May type — but also the air to which it was sung:

The lines were taken from some notes on Waterford made about 1543 by a Dr. Meredith Hammer, a Protestant clergyman, which are — as Dr. O'Driscoll's reference indicates — included among the Irish State Papers for the period in the unaccountable way in which such things tend to happen. The translation is interlined with the original Irish, transcribed phonetically in English script. An invigorating bout of wrestling with Dr. Hammer's handwriting and rendering of Irish sounds will produce something like this:

Rachaidh mise is rachaidh tusa go Fine Gall;
Iosfaidh mise, íosfaidh tusa gach a ngabhfam ann;
Goidfidh mise is goidfidh tusa gacha mart a bhfaghfam
ann ramhar;
Crochfar mise agus crochfar tusa agus cad a dhéanfaid
ár gclann?
Nuair fhasfaid fiacla acu féin éiríd fan ngleann !

We should also, as can be seen, amend slightly the English version published by Dr. O'Driscoll. The last line of the rhyme proper should read as I have it above, and the following addition — in brackets also in the manuscript — must be taken as comment.

The entire series of episodes is to my mind a quite staggering example of the durability of that tradition which Samuel Ferguson probably did more to rescue from annihilation than almost any other figure in the history of the literary reassertion of an Irish identity. It will be noted that the original English translator gives a praiseworthily fair version and refrains from superimposing on it any of that 'civilitie', the lack of which among the native Irish was so deplored by Spenser. Perhaps our greatest debt to Ferguson — and to those other inspired translators who were to follow him — is that by sheer integrity of intellect and sensitivity of appreciation they delivered an almost miraculously re-emergent Irish language from the cloying toils of a well-meant 'civilitie' which bade fair to strangle it at the hands of its most devoted professed admirers. One is reminded, in the context of our indomitable little nursery rhyme, of Auden's lines on Freud:

> All that he did was to remember
> Like the old and be honest like children.

The moral of this anecdote, it seems to me, is that of all the qualities, that most essential to the art of the translator is surely generosity. It is generosity to care enough about a hostile native population to find out what they are singing. Dr. Hammer's generosity was perhaps somewhat acerbic, yet he has left us in his debt. However, it is necessary to emphasise that it must also be an informed generosity. I am confident that this is equally the message behind Dr. O'Driscoll's analysis of the significance of Ferguson, one might say the text of his sermon — for, like all good literary criticism, this essay is almost overtly moral and didactic. It makes me happy to put on record that in the case of one reader at least the sermon was preached to the converted and the converted were enchanted to listen. In demonstrating the aptitudes of head and heart, which so peculiarly fitted his subject to reconcile two divergent traditions so that a new flowering might ensue from the graft, Dr. O'Driscoll has shown incidentally the considerable degree to which he partakes himself of the same humane and scholarly attributes.

MÁIRE CRUISE O'BRIEN

AN ASCENDANCY OF THE HEART

I

Towards the end of Robert Louis Stevenson's *The Wrecker* we are introduced to an Ulsterman named Mac. Mac has just assaulted an Australian for calling him an Irishman:

> "But you *are* an Irishman, aint you?" . . .
> "I may be," says Mac, "but I'll allow no Sydney duck to call me so. No," he added, with a sudden heated countenance, "nor any Britisher that walks !" [1]

Writing in 1911, George Birmingham claimed that Mac was a characteristic nineteenth-century Ulster Protestant.[2] In the light of Birmingham's generalisation, the following words by another nineteenth-century Ulsterman are indeed startling: 'I am an Irishman and a Protestant,' Samuel Ferguson writes, but 'I was an Irishman before I was a Protestant.'[3] Although a Belfast Unionist, Ferguson, during the 1830's, initiated an attempt to reconcile the two religious communities that constitute the Irish nation. This reconciliation was to be effected through education, cultural nationalism, the cultivation of mutual respect for the distinctive literary and historical traditions that had shaped the two communities, and the creation of a national literature. A national literature using Celtic myth for subject and taking its style from poetry written in the Irish language would, Ferguson argued, not only be the means of realizing the destiny he considered rightfully Ireland's, but would provide a link between people of diverse convictions: between Orange and Green, Protestant and Catholic, aristocrat

15

and peasant. Ferguson was successful in laying the foundations for an Irish national literature, but the apparent failure of this literature to bridge the divisions in Irish society is of more than historical interest. These divisions are, as we know, as real and as bitter today as they were in Ferguson's time. That Ferguson should, however, have made the attempt to reconcile the two communities gives his career an interest as much for the student of contemporary Irish affairs as for the literary historian.

Ferguson was born in 1810 into a Belfast where the ideals of the United Irish Society still lingered. This Society had been formed in 1791 and had proposed as its chief objects the creation of 'a brotherhood of affection, an identity of interests, a communion of rights, and a union of power among Irishmen of all religious persuasions.' The Society sought also to achieve 'impartial and adequate representation of the Irish nation in Parliament,'[4] but it was broken as a political force in 1795, and as a military one in 1798. Later, however, its principles were altered from a political to an educational ideal, for in 1810 the writer of the original prospectus of the Society, William Drennan, founded with others the Belfast Academical Institution, setting down as one of its aims the encouragement of communication between 'pupils of all religious denominations . . . by frequent and friendly intercourse, in the common business of education, by which means a new turn might be given to the national character and habits, and all the children of Ireland should know and love each other.'[5] What Drennan is proposing here is the union of Irishmen without regard to religion or class through social interchange and education, and what is relevant and interesting in the proposal is that it was being advanced by Belfast Protestants before Catholic Emancipation. From an educational to a literary ideal seems, in the hindsight of history, a natural transition. This was attempted by one of the pupils of the Academical Institution, by Ferguson, who advocated that the most effective way of dissipating the prejudices of his countrymen was by diverting their attention from the divided present in order to concentrate on the cultural and intellectual possibilities for the future.

Ferguson begins his literary career by confronting the problem of being a Protestant in a predominantly Roman Catholic country. In 'A Dialogue between the Head and Heart of an Irish Protestant', published in November 1833, he explores his ambivalent feelings towards his Catholic countrymen. To the Head of an Irish Protestant, he argues, the Roman Catholic Church seems simply a mixture of error and superstition :

> between the outworks of trick and legerdemain, and the citadel of church supremacy what a wilderness of error inexplicable — what pitfalls, traps, and labyrinths — what sloughs and stenches of superstition ! But, above all and beyond all, what a rampart in the deluded people's love? For the Irish priesthood hold the hearts of their seduced victims in even firmer bondage than in their minds.[6]

Irish Protestants, the Heart contends, are 'the controllers of popery; the safeguards of British connection; the guarantees of the empire's integrity; the most respectable body of men . . . in all Europe, whether we be considered with regard to wealth, industry, intellect, position, or absolute power' (II, 586). Yet the Heart feels betrayed: by centralising power and wealth in London, England was stripping the Kingdom of Ireland of its position and privilege, and England, the Heart warns, must be careful lest in its treatment of Ireland as a conquered colony it would alienate the very people who alone could preserve the British influence. The Heart too can admire the courage of its Roman Catholic countrymen who, however misapplied their loyalties, doggedly adhered to their religious principles through generations of adversity and oppression:

> I confess, were I myself the heart of an Irish Roman Catholic (and many thousands good as I beat in the hearts of Popish Irishmen,) it would claim all your influence to make me withdraw that support, however evidently misapplied. They have fasted for it [their religion], fought for it, suffered confiscation, exile, and death for it; through good and ill they have been constant and true to this; and the human heart cannot deny some charity to such devotedness. . . . I cannot argue. I only feel that, in the heart of a mere Irishman, I would have rebelled against the forced favour. (II, 590-91)

The Heart confesses a love of the land, and a Christian love of its Roman Catholic compatriots, for the sake of the human qualities evidenced in their loyalty to their traditions and religion:

> I love this land better than any other. I cannot believe it a hostile country. I love the people of it, in spite of themselves, and cannot feel towards them as enemies. . . . I cannot give up the nature of humanity, but I were

18

unworthy the heart of a Christian could I not submit to
some self-sacrifice for the Lord's sake. I still love my
Popish countrymen. I love them so much, that I would
bear the pain of seeming their error's persecutor, (and
they and error are so closely linked, that such a
character were little different from what the world calls
an oppressor,) for the sake of being able to love them
absolutely as free, loyal, and united Protestants.

(II, 591-3)

The Head, however, is less sympathetic. Irish Protestants, it claims, owe to the British Government the
protection of their lives and property, the preservation
of order and law. Concession to Catholic aspirations
would mean ultimate ruin for the nation, the confis-
cation of property, the constant possibility of war,
and the establishment of a foreign Church in Ireland.
Nurturing a vain hope that the Reformation would
yet happen in Ireland and rectify the impossible situation, the Head is apprehensive lest Roman Catholics
should succeed in their design to make Irish Protestants so disgusted with England that they would join
in the repeal of a union that it considered essential for
national security. If Catholic Emancipation should
produce repeal of the Union, the Head argues, 'so
surely will repeal produce ultimate separation; and so
sure as we have a separation, so surely will there be
war levied, estates confiscated, and the Popish church
established' (II, 588).

It is from Ferguson's head, from an intellectual defence of abstract principles, that certain early poems
emanate, instinctive, almost irresponsible, youthful
effulgences on the privileges of Protestantism, his dis-
trust of the Catholic clergy, and his disgust at constant

attempts at rebellion. Witness the opening stanzas of his 'Inaugural Ode' for the year 1834:

I

Oh ! friends be firm, and gather to one head
  Under our banner. Though a slender band,
And the breach'd rampart rocks beneath our tread,
  Yet bold and loyal here we make our stand,
  For God's dear love and sacred Ireland,
Against the leaguer of this subtle foe,
  Who, while he holds to heaven one impious hand
In mock appeal, works sinister below
  To raise a Papal throne on Britain's overthrow.

II

Here in our battle's vanguard have we planted
  The flag of freedom on the rock of ages :
Rally around it, ye, who yet undaunted
  By threats emblazoned on proscription's pages,
  Cast in the briber's teeth the apostate's wages
Which some once honourable hands defile;
  Stand for the cause of patriots and sages,
Nor heed the traitor's praise, nor flatterer's smile
  So as ye serve the truth and your lov'd native isle.

III

How dear we love our fair and famous island,
  Let the unbidden tears which ever rise
With dewy valley green, or azure highland,
  As first they open on our longing eyes
  After a sojourn under other skies,
Witness ! — Let each loch, river, glen, and grove,
  Which we have sworn and sought to immortalise,
Witness, how dearly all earth else above,
Thee, land of song and sighs, lorn Ireland, we love !

(III, vii)

A year earlier, in four immature self-congratulatory pieces of political doggerel, more significant for the sentiments they express than for any intrinsic merit, his tone is as uncompromising and more insulting: the Roman Catholics he considers 'jackasses', subvertors of State, Church, Law, and King:

> Oh for a hangman bold,
> Worthy our flag to hold,
> Onward to lead us 'gainst order and law!
> Loud would Clan Donkey then
> Ring from its loudest den,
> Glory and freedom for ever! — ee-aw!
> Ee-aw!
> Plunder and pillage for ever! — ee-aw!
>
> Hang out your rags on the infidels' Upas tree,
> Root and branch dripping with poison and blood —
> Blasphemy, treachery, treason, and sophistry,
> These are the fruits, and they prove the true good!
> Rooted in sin and lust
> Deep in our hearts, it must
> Flourish, while strength from a vice it can draw;
> Virtue shall all around
> Pine o'er the poisoned ground,
> While we sing Reason for ever! — ee-aw!
> Ee-aw!
> Reason and rapine for ever! — ee-aw! [7]

He contrasts the ragged traitors who gather beneath the French Republican Tricolour with the Protestant gentlemen, strong 'in the sacred might/Of Truth's eternal laws', who gather beneath the British banner:

> See, see, where the rags of the Tricolour brave us;
> Behold what a crew 'neath its tatters advance —
> Fools, tyrants, and traitors, in league to enslave us,
> A rabble well worthy the Ensign of France!

21

But up with the banner, let loyal breath fan her,
   She'll blaze o'er the heads of our gentlemen still —
Ho, Protestants, rally from mountain and valley,
   Around the old flagstaff on Liberty's hill !

Through the Broad Stone of Honour, the flagstaff is founded
   Deep, deep, in the sure Rock of Ages below;
It stood where rebellion's wild tempest resounded,
   'Twill stand, by God's will, though again it should blow !

On one thing, however, both the Head and Heart
of the Irish Protestant were united, and that was in
their love of Ireland, in their belief that their blood
was as genuinely Irish as a Catholic O'Driscoll or
O'Brien. The Ferguson family had come from Scotland
early in the seventeenth century, but the Presbyterian
planter, Ferguson argues, was only 'returning to the
land that sent him forth,' Ireland having colonised
Scotland many centuries earlier, and neither the in-
dignities they suffered at the hands of the centralising
Whigs in England, nor the suspicion and envy with
which they were regarded by their Popish countrymen
could deprive them 'of their birthright, which is the
love of Ireland' (II, 589). A man may be 'an Orange-
man, and neither a flatterer nor a betrayer,' Ferguson
writes, 'a Protestant gentleman may hate the Pope,
and yet be a more honest Irishman than the most
abject truckler to the priest, and most scornful vitu-
perator of the people' (III, 261).

The picture Ferguson presents of his Catholic
countrymen in his early immature poems, although
camouflaged by high spirits and youthful humour, is
therefore not a complimentary one : he refers to them
as fools, tyrants, traitors, jackasses, the puppets of

empire-building priests, militants against law and order. But his heart ultimately triumphs. For although Ferguson's fear of Popish domination was great, his love of Ireland was greater. Consequently, in 1833, his interest in the spiritual welfare of his country was such as to lead him to make an investigation of the literary legacy of his Catholic countrymen. With this intention in mind, he began to familiarise himself with the Irish language. He had not, while at the Academical Institution, been given an opportunity to study Irish, since classes in the language ceased there with William Nielson's death in 1821 and were not resumed until 1833.[8] Ferguson, however, formed a private class with two friends, George Fox and Thomas O'Hagan, to study the language.[9] By May 1833 he was still only a 'grammar scholar in Irish';[10] but by September of the same year he had acquired enough familiarity with the language to carry out his investigation.[11] The result was an analysis of Irish poetry, published in the *Dublin University Magazine* in 1834, which is one of the most significant and original pieces of literary criticism in nineteenth-century Ireland. To my mind these essays, and the accompanying translations of Irish poems, mark the beginning of the movement that was to culminate in the creation of a distinctive Irish literature in English, and since the essays have never been reprinted I shall quote, when necessary, extensively and frequently from them.

In these articles Ferguson provides for the first time in Anglo-Irish literary history an authentic analysis of the distinctive qualities of poetry in the Irish language. He also explores the national characteristics of the people who had given this literature to the world. The essays are essays of discovery and wonder and hope, as a rich new tradition, which he had never suspected to exist, unfolds itself before his imagination : 'Our readers,' he writes, 'have, in the translated parts of these pages, read such writing as they have never read before; and many, we would hope, have obtained glimpses of the character of a people, such as they never before knew or cared for' (III, 477). It is true that Ferguson writes as one of the ascendancy, and in his initial declarations of sympathy for the repressed Catholic Irish there is a touch of arrogant condescension. But as he probes deeper into the character of the poetry and people he begins, to his own surprise, to regard them as equals and as integral to the spirit of the nation. His prejudices dissipate, as he perceives for the first time a solution to the Irish problem, a practical means of bringing together two groups of Irishmen that had long been separated. Instead of allowing the self-interested politician or anarchist the opportunity to capitalise on the internal divisions that history had created, the two peoples that constituted the nation could, through education, learn mutual toleration and respect :

> We will not suffer two of the finest races of men in the world, the Catholic and Protestant, or the Milesian and Anglo-Irish, to be duped into mutual hatred by the tale-bearing go-betweens who may struggle in impotent malice against our honest efforts, even though the panders of dissension should be willing to pay out of their own pockets — as some, who may look to their backs and shoulders, have done — for the satisfaction of setting us by our ears. But let it first be our task to make the

people of Ireland better acquainted with one another. We address in these pages the Protestant wealth and intelligence of the country, an interest acknowledged on all hands to be the depository of Ireland's fate for good or evil. The Protestants of Ireland are wealthy and intelligent beyond most classes, of their numbers, in the world : but their wealth has hitherto been insecure, because their intelligence has not embraced a thorough knowledge of the genius and disposition of their Catholic fellow-citizens. The genius of a people at large is not to be learned by the notes of Sunday tourists. The history of centuries must be gathered, published, studied and digested, before the Irish people can be known to the world, and to each other, as they ought to be. We hail, with daily-increasing pleasure, the spirit of research and liberality which is manifesting itself in all the branches of our national literature, but chiefly in our earlier history and antiquities—subjects of paramount importance to every people who respect, or even desire to respect themselves. Let us contribute our aid to the auspicious undertaking, and introduce the Saxon and Scottish Protestant to an acquaintance with the poetical genius of a people hitherto unknown to them, as being known only in a character incompatible with sincerity or plain dealing. (III, 457)

The picture of the Catholic Irish that had been presented to the world, the depiction of them as creatures of blind anger and ludicrous folly, or as niggling nuisances and embarrassments to the Kingdom, was, Ferguson discovered, a false one which had been created by exploiters of their deprivation and good-will. Ferguson found instead that the true genius of the Catholic Irish had been expressed in poems 'such as the speakers of the English language at large have never heard before' (IV, 153), in a literature addressed not to sophisticated audiences of drawing-rooms, theatres, or political platforms, but written solely for the ear of beloved or patron, or to alleviate the moods of a burdened heart. In this literature, cloaked to that point in time in the obscurity of the Irish tongue or presented in English as an antiquarian curiosity, Ferguson could discern the qualities that constituted the heart of the Catholic nation : pride in genealogy, respect for courage, a tendency and power to mythologise people and places, fervour, hospitality, courtesy, idealisation of woman, sanctity of place and love of tradition, a sense of the wonder and beauty of the land presented side by side with the naked realities of material existence. These are songs which are fresh and original and graceful, songs not addressed to the intellect or judgment but which appeal directly to the heart. We can look in vain, Ferguson argues, for the qualities which have passed as characteristic of Irish poetry in previous translations from the Irish, or in the original words which accompanied Moore's *Melodies*: 'the chasteness, the appositeness, the anti-thetical and epigrammatic point, and the measured propriety of prosody, which delight the ear and the judgment' (IV, 153). It was the very simplicity and spontaneity of the songs that constituted their attraction as poetry and as keys to Irish sentiment and to customs that history had obliterated.

Ferguson concentrated his analysis on three types of poems : panegyrics, poems of dispossession, and love songs. He was impressed by the good-will, sincerity and extravagance of stylized panegyrics celebrating the beauty or liberality of patrons, especially those of Carolan, who, although primarily a musician, was ingenious enough to accompany his music with words designed to gratify the fancy of a patron. Ferguson made several literal translations of Carolan's poems to demonstrate the bard's ingenuity in finding some subject for praise in each of his innumerable claimants, his insight into many varieties of rank and character, the excellence of the poetic composition usually varying directly with the interest he took in his subject.[12] It is interesting that when Ferguson republishes some of these translations in *The Lays of the Western Gael* more than thirty years later, the playful high spirits and first flush of enthusiasm that he had experienced in 1834 has been subdued by a sense of the sophisticated literary audience to which he is now presenting them :

> The office of the bard required skill in music, a retentive memory, and a knowledge of the common forms of panegyric rather than original genius. A large proportion of these compositions consisted of adulatory odes addressed to protectors and patrons. Many of the best musical performances of Carolan are associated with works of this character, and exhibit an incongruous union of noble sounds and mean ideas. It has been usual, in giving him and the later harpers the credit which they well merit for originality and fertility in the production of melodies, to include their odes and songs, as efforts of poetic genius, in the commendation; but these portions of the compositions are generally made up of gross flatteries and the conventionalities of the Pantheon. The images and sentiments are in all much alike; and it is rarely that an original thought repays the trouble of the translator. In celebrating some of the ladies of families who patronized him, Carolan has, however,

produced a few pieces in which the words are not unworthy of the music. He was sensible of the charms of grace and virtue, and although incapable of distinguishing between elegant and vulgar forms of praise, has in these instances expressed genuine sentiments of admiration with a great degree of natural and affectionate tenderness — united, it must be remembered, with original and beautiful music.[13]

More moving to Ferguson are the intense expressions of loyalty by the hereditary bards who by their passionate and patriotic verses roused the Catholic nobility to take arms against their oppressors. His literal translation of 'O'Hussey's Ode' captures the savage power that permeates the vivid and vigorous descriptions of the original, while his finished translations of 'The Downfall of the Gael', 'O'Byrne's Bard to the Clans of Wicklow', and 'Lament over the Ruins of the Abbey of Timoleague', although lacking the fresh originality of his translations of love poems, capture the passionate feelings that permeate the original lamentations.

Ferguson's evocation of the effects of dispossession and of the independent spirit that fired the bards must have been surprising to himself, so contemptuous had he been a short time before of the constant Catholic attempts at rebellion. Through these bardic remains he becomes interested in the heroic exploits of previous Catholic leaders and goes on to depict those in his series of stories based on Irish history, *Hibernian Nights' Entertainments*. Of course, his spirit responded to that hopeless quality which moves these poems and so much of his own later poetry, the attraction of a lost cause. There must, however, have again been a division between his heart and head: his heart was captivated by the courage of the dispossessed hero and bard, his head by the knowledge that if they had succeeded, Ireland would no longer be a part of Great Britain.

But the poems which most allured Ferguson, and which he took most pride in presenting to the world, were the love poems of the seventeenth and eighteenth centuries, songs that did not parade the 'artificial pedantries' of the professional poet, but the 'simple sincerity' of the rustic lover (IV, 165). Ferguson was attracted by the fresh unstudied quality of these songs produced by humble poets living close to nature, the Irish lover promising no more than love or constancy, but promising them 'as man never did before' (IV, 166). He was moved by the original quality of the emotion, the intensity of the desire expressed, the apparent incurability of the passion, and the determination that it would not cease until death. The unique qualities that characterised the songs—despair, desire, a lack of licentiousness side by side with a sense of abandonment — Ferguson saw as linked to a poetic consciousness of national as well as personal loss:

> there is nothing impure, nothing licentious in their languishing but savage sincerity. This is the one great characteristic of all the amatory poetry of the country; and in its association with the despondency of conscious degradation, and the recklessness of desperate content, is partly to be found the origin of that wild, mournful, incondite, yet not uncouth, sentiment which distinguishes the national songs of Ireland from those of perhaps any other nation in the world. (IV, 154)

29

Humour, that catharsis for the discomfort of daily living, that public front by which the Irishman masks his private discontent, is not as characteristic of these national songs as pathos, a sense of irrevocable loss, and a knowledge that that loss can never be rectified: 'Desire is the essence of that pathos — desire either for the possession of love unenjoyed, or for the continuance of love being enjoyed, or for the restoration of enjoyed love lost' (IV, 155). Several of Ferguson's translations deal with each state. 'Pastheen Finn', 'The Coolun', 'The Fair-Hair'd Girl', 'Uileacan Dubh O', and 'Kitty Tyrrell' present poignant expressions of desire for the possession of a love yet unrealised:

Love of my heart, my fair Pastheen !
Her cheeks are red as the rose's sheen,
But my lips have tasted no more, I ween,
Than the glass I drank to the health of my queen !
   Then, Oro, come with me ! come with me ! come with me !
   Oro, come with me ! brown girl, sweet !
   And, oh ! I would go through snow and sleet,
   If you would come with me, brown girl, sweet !

                    (*Lays*, pp. 204-5)

'Cashel of Munster', 'Cean Dubh Deelish', 'The Dear Old Air', and another version of 'The Coolun' plead for the continuance of love already realised, even though the poet is aware that the experience of love will be transitory. Three translations—'Molly Astore', 'The Lapful of Nuts', and 'Nora of the Amber Hair' — are concerned with the restoration of love lost, while in 'Hopeless Love' and 'Mary's Waking' the poet expresses his acceptance of rejection by the beloved.[14] The quaint and pleasing 'Youghal Harbour' shows that sometimes the spurned poet is willing to offer everything he can, even marriage, to win the acceptance of the maiden :

> "My heart and hand here ! I mean you marriage !
>   I have loved like you and known love's pain;
> And if you turn back now to Youghal Harbour,
>   You ne'er shall want house or home again :
> You shall have a lace cap like any lady,
>   Cloak and capuchin, too, to keep you warm,
> And if God please, maybe, a little baby,
>   By and bye, to nestle within your arm."
>
> (*Lays*, p. 215)

But usually the lover holds out to the beloved, as Synge's tramps were to do later, the wild allurement of natural beauty. The lady, however, as the following unrhymed translation of 'Uileacan Dubh O' shows, was not always as liberated as Synge's heroines:

> If you would go with me to the County Leitrim,
>   Uileacan dubh O !
> I would give you the honey of bees and mead as food for you;
>   Uileacan dubh O !
> I shall give you the prospect of ships, and sails, and boats,
> Under the tops of the trees, and we returning from the strand,
> And I would never let any sorrow come upon you.
>   Oh ! you are my Uileacan dubh O !
>
> I shall not go with you, and it is in vain you ask me;
>   Uileacan dubh O !
> For your words will not keep me alive without food :
>   Uileacan dubh O !
> A thousand times better for me to be always a maid,
> Than to be walking the dew and the wilderness with you :
> My heart has not given to you love nor affection,
>   And you are not my Uileacan dubh O !
>
> (IV, 154)

Unlike most early lyrics, the promise of wealth or splendour is not held out in these poems as an additional inducement to the maiden to accept the hand of the possessor. The Irish lover alludes unconcernedly to his poverty, believing the admission to be in no way detrimental to his offer:

My purse holds no red gold, no coin of the silver white,
No herds are mine to drive through the long twilight!
But the pretty girl that would take me, all bare though I be
    and lone,
Oh, I'd take her with me kindly to the county Tyrone.

(Lays, p. 210)

Of course, the poet's admission of his state of poverty was sometimes necessary before he could be confident enough in his own sincerity to ask his beloved 'to walk the dews with him and live on mead and honey, or to take up her lodging with the black cocks and moor hens on the mountains' (IV, 166).

Although the thought, imagery, and pattern of these poems were similar, Ferguson refused to alter or sophisticate their simple sentiments. Most of the poems contain a description of the physical beauty of the beloved followed by a poignant expression of the poet's desire for union with her. These descriptions vary little from poem to poem: the maiden's neck is always more graceful than the swan; her bosom whiter than the apple blossom; her cheeks red as the rose, or the berry on the bough, or the rising sun; her hair either amber, golden, or flaxen, ringletted like branches, sweeping the tie of her sandal, or 'floating on the silken wing of the breeze'; and her voice sweeter than the magic sounds of fairy music, or the blackbird singing 'farewell to the setting sun'.

These descriptions of the physical beauty of the beloved only serve in impressing on the poet how victimised he is by her. The expression of love usually following the physical description is sincere, direct, and touched by the despair that comes from the knowledge of certain rejection.

I shall examine Ferguson's translations from the Irish later, but what is interesting here is not only his discovery of an authentic Irish literary tradition, but his determination to analyse the quality of the people who produced this tradition. Instead of a literature of self-indulgence and self-recrimination, as perhaps one could expect from a conquered people, the Catholic Irish had produced fervent marching songs, ingenious panegyrics that implied a sense of loyalty and patronage, fresh love songs in which pure desire and a genuine love of the country was expressed. This national poetry, too, possessed the key to an oral tradition and to living customs that stretched back through the centuries.

From his analysis of the qualities of Irish poetry, Ferguson is led to the arresting question: 'What constitutes a state?' Neither commerce nor industry, he asserts, but the quality of the people: 'if the men be cowards, and the women wantons, it were better a desert. On the other hand, people the desert with bold men and chaste women, and you have the elements of a nation, though its metropolis be a kraal, and its *via regia* a sheep track' (IV, 447). Ferguson was filled with surprise that the people who had created this national poetry had, despite the degradation of conquest, the constant attempts to undermine their self-respect, and the 'lingering tyranny of a debasing priest-craft', preserved their integrity as a people and a nation. Seven centuries of deprivation had not robbed the native Irish of what he considered their greatest asset, their virtue, and with it their love, 'their divine prompter of song'; and as neither ignorance, nor superstition, nor the 'brutalizing exclusion from humane society' had been successful in extinguishing this virtue, neither did he think that the knowledge, power, or luxury of more prosperous times would extinguish it. The discovery of these national qualities leads Ferguson to an over-romantic idealised view of the same women and men whom he had regarded with suspicion and contempt just a few months earlier:

> Our people, we believe, before Heaven, to be as brave and as virtuous a people as the world ever saw. Female purity is ever the concomitant, the crown and halo of true love; and the sentiment of legitimate desire . . . is not more nationally characteristic of our courageous countrymen, than is this its purer, though twin sister, attribute, of the virgins, wives, and matrons, whom we rejoice to call our fair and merry countrywomen.
>
> (IV, 447)

The adulation of manly courage and female purity may be considered to be abstract over-simplifications, but it is interesting that the same idealisation of woman was as deep-rooted in the Catholic Irish when they considered Synge's *Playboy of the Western World* as a slander against Irish women more than eighty years later.

Throughout his investigations, however, Ferguson discovers more precise qualities of the native Irish in which he takes pride: loyalty, hospitality, open-heartedness, gaiety, heroic aspirations, strong poetic feeling, patronage for poets, a capacity for indolence, an appreciation of the wild beauty of the country, a sense of the traditions that haunted their monumental antiquities. Their determination to retain these qualities through centuries of discord and deprivation earns Ferguson's highest respect. So much does he value these newly-discovered virtues that if Ireland could only attain to 'power and distinction . . . by forfeiting these qualities which have hallowed her adversity, we would rather see her chained for ever to the level of her present civil degradation' (IV, 447). It is vain, he argues, for would-be defenders of the Irish, writing with a more sophisticated English audience in mind, to attempt to explain away those qualities. For the same qualities which the defenders were careful to cloak made the Catholic peasant the attractive creature he was. Ferguson is careful to point out that the native Irish are a different people from the native English, and that their characteristics as a nation can never be altered or eradicated:

> we believe that [the] great proportion of the characteristics of a people are inherent, not fictitious; and that there are as essential differences between the genius's [sic] as between the physical appearances of nations. We believe that no dissipating continuance of defeat, danger, famine, or misgovernment, could ever, without the absolute infusion of Milesian blood, Hibernicize the English peasant; and that no stultifying operation of mere security, plenty, or laborious regularity could ever, without actual physical transubstantiation, reduce the native Irishmen to the stolid standard of the sober Saxon.
> (IV, 154-5)

It is partly a matter of blood and physical geo-graphy, partly a matter of race and nationality, but as George Bernard Shaw and Roger Casement were to discover later, there is something more: 'There is something in the soil, in the air, in the inherited mind of a country that is as real, nay more real, than the rocks, the hills and the streams. No historian defines the thing, yet it exists in all lands — and in Ireland its influence has never failed.' [15]

The most distinctive quality Ferguson discovers in the Catholic nation, that of loyalty to family and clan, potentially their greatest asset, had proved through history to be their greatest liability. For instead of the great families uniting under a common head to repel the English invaders and re-establish the independence of the nation, as they could easily have done in the earlier centuries, they dissipated their energies in civil strife: 'Had these [patriarchal] principles been per-mitted to attain their legitimate extension, the nation might have been united and independent; but, hin-dered by the very vigour of their own growth, those seeds of a legitimate loyalty ran to waste in the wild and thorny entanglement of factious clanship, instead of shaping themselves into the simple strength of individual monarchy' (IV, 448). It is to the excess of this quality, natural piety, or the principle of patriar-chal loyalty in its narrowest application, that Ferguson traces the tardiness of Irish society to develop beyond a 'shepherd' state:

> It is to the excess of natural piety, developing itself in over loyal attachments to principles subversive of reason and independence, that we would trace the tardiness,

nay, sometimes the retrogression of civilization and prosperity in Ireland. Natural piety we would define as the religion of humanity, the faith of the affections, the susceptibility of involuntary attachments to arbitrary relations in society, that constitution of character most favourable to legitimate religious impressions, were it not that its super-abundance of devotion too often runs to waste on sublunary or superstitious and dissipating objects. The Irish are by nature preeminently pious. . . .

(IV, 448)

The Catholic people are in short a people of excess, a people of instinct, veneration, and emotion rather than a people of considered intellect or reason. Only the Roman Catholic Church had succeeded in harnessing their preeminent piety and loyalty, their natural instinct for reverence. Qualities that were essential in building a mature nation were therefore spent in supernatural attachments and in undermining a constitution and law that must, according to Ferguson, form the basis of a secure state. It is interesting that Synge later was able to produce some of his startling literary effects by playing up exactly those same qualities that Ferguson was condemning, the innate disrespect among the Irish for British constitution and law. Nevertheless Ferguson was writing in a different historical period, with different assumptions, and seeking a compromise and redirection of energy where, perhaps, no compromise or redirection was possible. It must be remembered too that the Irish disrespect for law was for a law that had been imposed on them, and that it was only by indifference and disrespect that they could preserve their spirit of independence. For their ancient Brehon laws, as Ferguson's researches were to prove later, and as he was to bring out in his later poems, 'Conary' for example, the Irish had the deepest respect and fear for the very letter of the law.

In 1834 Ferguson is writing with certain assumptions that were the natural result of his background and temperament. The fact that the native Irish people are different from the British people is clear to him, but the notion of an independent Ireland does not cross his mind. Like Edmund Burke, his assumption is that Ireland is part of an 'imperial confederacy', and like Burke, he assumes that the British development of constitutional monarchy is an ideal development. He is correct, however, in discerning two stages of society in Ireland, existing side by side. He could see, on the one hand, the remnants of a patriarchal society which was partly the result of the adoption of an Irish mode of existence by the original Norman invaders. On the other hand, the British settlers in Ireland believed in a society modelled on the political progress of England, where a feudal society developed and was followed, after the revolution of 1688, by the establishment of a strong constitutional monarchy. What Ferguson regarded as regrettable was that the Irish as a whole had not adopted what seemed to him the superior form of British government. He assumed too that the particular stages of government through which England had progressed were necessary stages in the evolution of a civilised country.

Successive English triumphs increased the division within the Irish, and also encouraged a separation between the native Irish themselves, between the over-privileged Irish within the Pale and the under-privileged Irish outside it. The Reformation widened the gulf even further, and the dogged adherence of the native Irish to the Roman Catholic Church cut any hope of reconciliation. The result was a sharp division in the temper and ideas of the Irish people:

> Thus it is that we have had no middle stage of society to conduct the people by just degrees through the natural progress of spontaneous civilization; this has been the reason why we find the principles of the revolution operating so inefficiently on a nation not yet free from the reluctant sway of patriarchal loyalty; and hence it has come to pass, that Irish society, at the present day, exhibits those anomalous features of mixed crudeness and maturity which are but the representatives of two different stages of society, whose antagonist principles have hitherto found no mutual means of reconcilement. (IV, 451)

Industrial prosperity could perhaps remove the economic barrier separating the Irish people; increased communication between classes could minimise the social barrier; religious toleration could perhaps be fostered. Ferguson, too, in his loyalist optimism, nurtured a hope that the native Irish would discover the virtue of constitutional monarchy and that the 'untutored loyalty of the clansman' could be carried forward 'until the whole country becomes his faction and the king his chief' (IV, 451). But the greatest division between the two different kinds of Irishmen, that created by temperament, the barrier between a people of emotion and a people of reason, could never be eradicated. Consequently, what was needed was mutual toleration, self-respect, education in the fullest sense, and more particularly in the scriptural sense:

> But are our people such as could make a nation of the
> desert, much more of such a rich and well-conditioned
> island? Education based upon the only true basis —
> scriptural education alone is wanted to make our men
> as bold as our women are chaste — to make us a nation
> of enlightened, liberal, and prosperous people—assertors
> of our own rights, respecters of the rights of others —
> a truly integral and influential portion of the empire,
> repudiating alike the insolent violence of civil degra-
> dation and the hideous impiety of spiritual thraldom —
> in the fullest sense of the words, bold men, honoured
> by others and respected by ourselves. . . . [T]o make
> Irishmen know themselves and one another; this is the
> want, this is the worthiest labour of the age. Education,
> in its fullest sense, is the engine by whose agency we
> hope to see the great work yet effected; and when we
> speak of education in the fullest sense, we mean not
> only the supply of useful and wholesome knowledge to
> the lower classes, but fearless exposure of the true
> temper, wants, and capabilities, of their tenantry and
> labourers, to the proprietors themselves of the land. May
> God grant our country a peaceful opportunity for the
> accomplishment of that blessed and meritorious work!
>   (IV, 448-51)

This essential self-knowledge could therefore be created among the Irish through education, not necessarily
through a study of their own century, where attitudes
had solidified to the point of impenetrability, but
through a study of former centuries, when qualities
of character were forming: 'The history of centuries
must be gathered, published, studied and digested,
before the Irish people can be known to the world,
and to each other, as they ought to be' (III, 457). The
Protestant ascendancy must embrace the traditions

of their Catholic countrymen; the capabilities and
legitimate desires of the Catholic Irish must be arti-
culated and understood. For what, traditionally, had
been a matter of contention, the diversity within the
nation, could be a matter of strength, and the qualities
of the two peoples could if properly applied form the
basis of an 'almost perfect' society :

> Alas that a nation glowing with the most enthusiastic
> courage, moved by the tenderest sympathies, and pene-
> trated by a constitutional piety as devoted as profound,
> should so long have misapplied those noblest attributes
> of a high-destined people ! What material for an almost
> perfect society does the national genius not present?
> Instinctive piety, to lay the only sure foundation of
> human morals and immortal hopes; constitutional loyal-
> ty, to preserve the civil compact inviolate; legitimate
> affection, to ensure public virtue and private happiness;
> endless humour, to quicken social intercourse; and last,
> and, save one attribute, best, indomitable love of country
> to consolidate the whole. (IV, 467)

Eight million people, Ferguson posits, cannot remain
forever in obscurity : 'sooner or later Ireland must
rise into importance, perhaps as an emulator, perhaps
as an equal, perhaps as a superior to the other mem-
bers of our imperial confederacy' (IV, 447).

Despite his paranoid fear of the Catholic clergy, his
suspicion of the 'ulterior' motives of the Roman
Catholic Church, his self-righteous assumption of the
superiority of constitutional monarchy, and his contempt for any endeavour to separate Ireland from the
confederacy of which he believed she was naturally a
part, Ferguson in these articles has travelled a long
distance. He has assessed the qualities of Ireland's

national poetry; he has perceived the integrity of the Catholic people who produced it, and he seems willing to accept them as co-equals of the Protestant ascendancy and as essential a part of the soul of the nation. Perhaps, when he began his investigation, he did not foresee where precisely he would be led, that what began as an intellectual curiosity would lead him into a passionately imaginative immersion in the past of his country. As Maire Mac an tSaoi has written, Ferguson ventures 'a long way into enemy country' and comes 'closer to them in his heart than clearly, as an enlightened Protestant gentleman of his day, he cares to admit. Language and antiquarianism have betrayed him; the material he approached as a scholarly pastime . . . has captured his imagination and will dominate all his subsequent literary achievement.' [16]

Ferguson used as the occasion for his investigation of Irish poetry the publication in 1831 of James Hardiman's *Irish Minstrelsy, or Bardic Remains of Ireland with English Poetical Translations*. He brought to his study of this volume independent research into published sources and unpublished manuscripts, and a thorough knowledge of the history, society, and cultural environment that produced the poems. He quarrels with some of Hardiman's historical assumptions and interpretations: the spirit of political and religious fanaticism that permeates the volume; the blanket defence of the Catholic clergy and the moral purity of all Irish literature; the attempts to camouflage characteristic qualities of the native Irish — their intemperance, their capacity for indolence, and their sense of abandonment. More importantly, Ferguson takes Hardiman to task for using the national poetry in order to gain a political 'monopoly of native Irish sympathies' (IV, 516), for standing, despite protestations to the contrary, between the native Irish and the Protestant ascendancy, and for harping on past aggravations rather than holding out the prospect of reconciliation through cultural collaboration.

For Hardiman's industry in preserving poems that would have been lost forever to succeeding generations, and especially for his presentation of the texts of the Irish originals, Ferguson has nothing but the highest praise. There is, too, lacking in Ferguson's attack any element of personal vindictiveness or bigotry, as the following unpublished letter demonstrates:

43

I have often felt since I first had the pleasure of knowing you personally, that your treatment of me as a friend, after the first petulant — tho' really not ill designed — attack on your first publication in which I had been engaged so shortly before, ought to give me a lesson of forbearance & good feeling in after life; and the consideration you show me, now, in presenting me with your last piece, renders it impossible for me to refrain from expressing that sentiment. I believe I would not have had occasion to make this acknowledgement if you had not perceived from my writings & conversation that, however we might differ on means, we agreed in an ardent desire for the same ends, the elevation of Irish literature, & the aggrandisement in all good gifts of the Irish people. It is vain to regret disagreements; but it is a satisfaction & pleasure to feel that there is one great, fixed, and blessed object in which all who are engaged become not only better citizens but kinder and gentler men. I hope, my dear Sir, that I may long see you labouring honestly in that field, and that I may yet live to do something in it myself that may show I was worthy to be treated by other good Irishmen with so much and so highly prized consideration.[17]

The Irish Minstrelsy is indeed the first comprehensive attempt to collect Irish popular poetry and represents as important a landmark in the history of Irish poetry as Edward Bunting's collection of national airs represents in the history of Irish music. Hardiman's first intention was simply to publish the Irish texts with a few explanatory notes. He then considered the possibility of literal English translations of the Irish originals, but 'the difficulty, or rather impossibility, of preserving the spirit of the bards; and the consequent injury to their works and memory' made him abandon this intention.[18] He was, however, in his own eyes, able to overcome these difficulties by entrusting the task of presenting 'his literal essayings in the more appropriate garb of verse' to some 'literary friends of acknowledged poetical abilities', Thomas Furlong, Henry Grattan Curran, William Hamilton Drummond, John D'Alton, and Edward Lawson. This was unfortunate in one sense, for in presenting verse translations of the type they did, James Hardiman and his translators fell into the trap of all previous translators of Irish poetry. It was, however, fortunate in another sense in that it spurred Ferguson to make his own translations in which he broke boldly with the established tradition.

While commending Hardiman for preserving his country's national songs, Ferguson censured him severely for including translations 'so strangely unlike the originals both in sentiment and style, as to destroy alike the originality and the interest of Irish minstrelsy for those who can only appreciate it through such a medium' (IV, 453). Although applauding the purpose, Ferguson condemned the execution, stating that all the translators were 'actuated by a morbid desire, neither healthy nor honest, to elevate the tone of the original to a pitch of refined poetic art altogether foreign from the whole genius and *rationale* of its composition.' Many of the translations he condemned as 'spurious, puerile, unclassical — lamentably bad', and each translator he dismissed with a disdain that is only alleviated by the good-humoured manner in which his criticism was expressed.

Translations from the Irish had been made before, the earliest surviving one being made in the sixteenth century :

45

You and I will go to Finegall.
You and I will eat such meats as we find there.
You and I will steal such beef as we find fat.
I shall be hanged and you shall be hanged. What shall our
children do?
When teeth do grow unto themselves as their fathers did
before?[19]

Edmund Spenser reveals in his *View of the Present State of Ireland* that his curiosity about the native tradition led him to have some Irish poems translated, but none of the translations survive. A short time later, in 1635, Michael Kearney translated into English an Irish poem on genealogy, 'The Kings of the Race of Eibhear', by John O'Dugan, and this poem seems to be the first verse translation of an Irish poem.

During the first part of the eighteenth century only a few translations of Irish poems were made. In 1720 Jonathan Swift wrote his *Description of an Irish-Feast* from a literal translation of an Irish poem furnished him by Hugh MacGaurin; and in 1723 Dermod O'Connor included in his translation of Geoffrey Keating's *General History of Ireland* English versions of the Irish poems Keating had quoted. In 1734 Francis Hutchinson stated in the Preface to his *Defence of the Antient Historians* that 'the Natives have of late translated many of their old Fragments in *English* Verse and Prose'; but he did not print any of the translations. A translation of an Irish song appeared in the *Gentleman's Magazine* in 1751[20] and was published later in Joseph Ritson's *Collection of English Songs* in 1783. Two translations from the Irish were published in the *European Magazine, and London Review* in 1782, the

46

first a prose literal version, and the second a sonnet translated by Edward Nolan. The rhymed translation is feigned and artificial, but the literal translation, although coloured with a typical eighteenth-century coquetry, preserves the freshness one would expect to find in the originals:

> It was on the white hawthorn, on the brow of the valley, I saw the ring of day first break.
> The soft, the young, the gay, delightful morning, kissed the crimson off the rose, mixed it with her smiles, and laughed the season on us.
> Rise, my Evelina, soul that informs my heart; do thou smile too, more lovely than the morning in her blushes, more modest than the rifled lily, when weeping in her dews. . . .
> Thy lover will pick thee strawberries from the lofty cragg, and rob the hazel of its yellow nuts. My berries shall be red as thy lips, and my nuts ripe and milky as the love-begotten fluid in the bridal bosom.[21]

During the last two decades of the eighteenth century, chiefly because of the influence of James Macpherson and his imputed 'translations', a greater interest was taken in Irish poetry. Books devoted entirely to its translation into English were published, the first being Charles Wilson's *Poems Translated from the Irish Language into the English* in 1782, the second being Charlotte Brooke's *Reliques of Irish Poetry* in 1789. Wilson also published some translations in his *Brookiana* in 1804, and four years later Theophilus O'Flanagan included some in the first volume of his *Transactions of the Gaelic Society of Dublin* in 1808. But while Wilson's translations attracted little attention, Charlotte Brooke's *Reliques* circulated widely in

47

England and Ireland.[22] Earlier, in 1786, Miss Brooke had published anonymously seven English translations of Irish poems in Joseph Cooper Walker's *Historical Memoirs of the Irish Bards*, a work which provided a general history of the Irish bards, a descriptive and historical account of ancient Irish musical instruments, anecdotes and observations on Irish music.

In 1796 Edward Bunting published his first collection of Irish music. As early as 1797 Thomas Moore's attention was directed to the collection. He approached Bunting and offered to write original words to accompany the airs. Bunting, however, rejected the proposal, and it was not until ten years later that Moore began to publish the first of his *Irish Melodies*. The qualities in the airs that Moore notes in his manifesto for the series are interesting: their erratic and puzzling mixture of levity and melancholy; their seemingly irregular and lawless metres, and the difficulty of reconciling these metres to the sober standards of taste which, he felt, the sophisticated literary public expected. Moore did not know Irish and consequently, not being able to translate the words of the songs that Bunting had published, he wrote his own words. Yeats dismisses Moore's *Melodies* as 'excellent drawing-room songs, pretty with a prettiness which is contraband of Parnassus.' Moore, Yeats contends, does not have 'distinction of style; his conventional phrases are too closely interwoven with their patriotism, his mechanical cadences too firmly married to the ancient music of their country.'[23] Yet Yeats under-estimates Moore's achievement. Moore was working chiefly from instinct, and it is a mark of his daring and genius that despite his handicaps he could introduce into English some of the real metrical features of the originals:

> At the mid hour of night, when stars are weeping, I fly
> To the lone vale we loved, when life shone warm in
> thine eye. . . .

Apart from style, what is perhaps more remarkable is that, though ignorant of the Irish language, Moore captures at times the substance as well as the spirit of the originals. In 'The Irish Peasant to his Mistress' we have, as in the Gaelic *aisling*, the personification of Ireland as the poet's mistress, and in many of the *Melodies* we have the haunting evocation of that lost glory, that sense of dispossession and deprivation that animates the Irish poems.

In 1809 Bunting published his second collection of Irish music and included nine translations of Irish poems by Mary Balfour (Miss Balfour also published a translation of 'The Maid of Brocah' in her *Hope, A Poetical Essay : with various other Poems* the following year), four by Thomas Campbell, and one each by William Drennan, John Brown, Hector Macneill, W. R. Spencer, and Baron Dawson. Bunting, however, was chiefly intent on the preservation of the music, and the interests of translation were consequently ruthlessly subordinated: words were produced which were not an accurate translation of the originals, but something which could easily be sung to the music. In all the poems of the principal translator, Miss Balfour, the originals are altered 'drastically so as to bring them into conformity with her ideal of Irish song — contemporary English drawing-room song mildly flavoured with Ossianism. Thus in her hands the Irish poems lose their vigour and directness; the personal note is replaced by a literary sentimentality and a conventional prettiness.'[24]

More sustained critical comment is necessary on the two most important books of translations, Charlotte Brooke's *Reliques* and those included in Hardiman's *Irish Minstrelsy*. Charlotte Brooke's *Reliques* is extremely significant in the history of Anglo-Irish translation, because despite its many drawbacks it focused considerable attention on Irish poetry and dissipated some of the suspicion and contempt with which it was then regarded. To counteract the prejudice surrounding Irish poetry, 'to throw some light on the antiquities of this country, to vindicate, in part, its history,' and 'in the hope of awakening a just and useful curiosity, on the subject of our poetical composition,'[25] she undertook her task of translating specimens of the bardic remains.

Miss Brooke possessed a genuine appreciation of the poems produced by the Irish bards. They exhibit, she writes, 'a glow of cultivated genius, — a spirit of elevated heroism, — sentiments of pure honour, — instances of disinterested patriotism, — and manners of a degree of refinement, totally astonishing, at a period when the rest of Europe was nearly sunk in barbarism.'[26] But in translating these poems into English she experienced a number of difficulties. First, she found that the capability of the Irish language 'to repeat the same thought, without tiring the fancy or the ear' produced in a faithful English translation 'a sameness, and repetition of thought'. Second, she found that the flexibility as well as the concentration of the Irish language made the task of the translator almost impossible :

> It is really astonishing of what various and comprehensive powers this neglected language is possessed. In the pathetic, it breathes the most beautiful and affecting simplicity; and in the bolder species of composition, it is distinguished by a force of expression, a sublime dignity, and rapid energy, which it is scarcely possible for any translation fully to convey; as it sometimes fills the mind with ideas altogether new, and which, perhaps, no modern language is entirely prepared to express. One compound epithet must often be translated by two lines of English verse, and, on such occasions, much of the beauty is necessarily lost; the force and effect of the thought being weakened by too slow an introduction on the mind; just as that light which dazzles, when flashing swiftly on the eye, will be gazed at with indifference, if let in by degrees.[27]

Miss Brooke was well aware of her own failings as a translator. Many times she apologises for her inadequacy to transfer faithfully the thought and expression of the Irish original to the English version. She felt that much of the simplicity and distinctive beauty of the originals was lost in translation : 'indeed, so sensible was I of this, that it influenced me to give up, in despair, many a sweet stanza to which I found myself quite unequal.'[28]

We do not find the same sensitivity either to the Irish originals, or to the problems of translation, in the Hardiman translators. When Thomas Furlong's aid was first solicited, James Hardiman reveals, 'the writer had the same difficulty with him, as with the others, to prove that any productions of value were extant in the Irish language. Acquainted only with the English words associated with our native airs, he smiled incredulously at the asserted poetical excellence of the original lyrics, and even questioned their existence. It was true, he admitted, that he had often heard them spoken of, and sometimes praised, but that he considered as the mere boasting of national prejudice. 'If,' said he, 'they possess any merit, I cannot conceive how they could have remained so long unknown.'[29] Furlong's incredulity when confronted with the originals and his method of translating them was the method best calculated to conceal their distinctive qualities: in his translations, he concedes, he 'endeavoured to express himself as he conceived the bard would have done, had he composed in English.'[30]

Like the Hardiman translators, Miss Brooke chose poetry rather than prose as the medium for her translations. To give a literal version, she felt, would do the originals a poetic injustice:

> I should have found that an impossible undertaking. — Besides the spirit which they breathe, and which lifts the imagination far above the tameness, let me say, the *injustice*, of such a task, — there are many complex words that could not be translated literally, without great injury to the original, — without being "false to the sense, and falser to its fame."[31]

Despite these reasons for not making literal versions, Miss Brooke did include one in her *Reliques*, 'Carolan's Song for Gracey Nugent'. It is ironic that it is this version, not the verse translation also given, nor indeed any of the other verse translations in the volume, that comes closest to representing in English the content of an Irish original. Ferguson also made a literal translation of the poem. By comparing his and Miss Brooke's, and the verse translations of Miss Brooke and Furlong, the qualities of each as a translator of Irish poetry can be demonstrated. Ferguson, with an eye for absolute accuracy, makes the lines in his literal version correspond to the lines in the original poem. Charlotte Brooke's literal translation is in prose, but to make it easier for comparison I have arranged her prose into lines that correspond to the lines of verse.

Ferguson's version is an accurate rendering of the content, tone, and some of the idioms of the original:

> It is my desire to treat of the blossom of whiteness;
> Grace, the sprightliest damsel:
> And she it was who had excellence in qualities and
> understanding
> Over the beautiful accomplished women of the province.
> Whoever would be near her by night and by day
> Need not fear ever long sorrow or suffering,
> With the gentle queen of happy dispositions.
> She is the Coolin of the branches and circles.
>
> Her side is as the lime, her neck is as the swan's,
> And her aspect is as the summer's sun:
> Is it not happy for him to whom was promised in his
> portion
> To be with her, the branch of bending tendrils?
>
> (III, 474)

Miss Brooke's prose version, although closer in content to the original than any of her verse translations, does not approach the accuracy of Ferguson's translation:

I will sing with rapture of the Blossom of Whiteness!
Gracey, the young and beautiful woman,
who bore away the palm of excellence in sweet manners
    and accomplishments,
from all the Fair-ones of the provinces.
    Whoever enjoys her constant society,
    no apprehension of any ill can assail him.
    — The Queen of soft and winning mind and
        manners,
    with her fair branching tresses flowing in ringlets.

Her side like alabaster, and her neck like the swan,
and her countenance like the Sun in summer.
How best it is for him who is promised, as riches,
to be united with her, the branch of fair curling
    tendrils.[32]

The original is utterly simple, direct, and concrete.
Miss Brooke, however, introduces abstractions and
generalised notions because her mind is accustomed
to a particular mode of eighteenth-century expression.
She introduces social notions (as 'whoever enjoys
her constant society' for 'Cia b'é bhiadh na h-aice
d'oídhche 's de ló', literally 'whoever would be beside
her by night and by day'); generalised abstractions
(as 'no apprehension of any ill can assail him' for
'Ní baéghal dó fad-thuirse choídhche ná brón', literally
'No danger to him long-suffering ever or sorrow');
clichéd metaphors (as 'who bore away the palm of
excellence' for ' 'S gur b'í rug bárr', literally 'she took
the top'); and substitutes polite words for the right
words (as 'alabaster' for 'aél', literally 'lime'). She
introduces thoughts not in the original (as 'with
rapture' in line 1), completes implied thought (as
'to be united to her' for 'bheith aici-si', literally 'to be

hers'), and has plain errors of translation (as 'young and beautiful' for 'an ainnfhir is súgaíche', literally 'the merriest maiden').

In her verse translation Miss Brooke takes further liberties with the simple thoughts of the original. She also chooses a stale stereotyped abstract language and a typical eighteenth-century form of versification, the rhyming couplet gathered into quatrains:

Of Gracey's charms enraptur'd will I sing!
Fragrant and fair, as blossoms of the spring;
To her sweet manners, and accomplish'd mind,
Each rival Fair the palm of Love resign'd.

How blest her sweet society to share!
To mark the ringlets of her flowing hair;
Her gentle accents, — her complacent mien! —
Supreme in charms, she looks — she reigns a Queen!

That alabaster form — that graceful neck,
How do the Cygnet's down and whiteness deck! —
How does that aspect shame the cheer of day,
When summer suns their brightest beams display.

Thomas Furlong, in his translation of the poem, chooses weak alternate rhyming, a language imitative of eighteenth-century poetic diction at its weakest and thinnest, and produces, not a simple panegyric for a patroness, as the original is, but a commonplace sentimental love poem in the weakest manner of the eighteenth century:

Oh! joy to the blossom of white-bosom'd maids,
  To the girl whose young glance is endearing,
Whose smile, like enchantment, each circle pervades,
  She who makes even loneliness cheering.

55

Oh ! he that beholds thee by night or day,
    He who seeks thee in beauty before him,
Tho' stricken and spell-bound may smile and say,
    That he blesses the charm that's o'er him.

Her neck is like snow, rich and curling her hair,
    Her looks like the sun when declining;
Oh ! happy is he who may gaze on the fair,
    While her white arms round him are twining. . . .[33]

It is clear, as comparison with Ferguson's literal translation will show, that Furlong has taken the most
blatant liberties with the original. Some of the Hardiman translations are even more flagrant abuses of the
content of the originals, embellishments designed to
impress a public ignorant of Irish poetry. Witness
John D'Alton's 'Torna's Lament for Corc and Niall':

Oh ! let me think in age
    Of years rolled by,
    When in the peace of infancy,
Mid all the ties of holy fosterage,
The future lords of Erin's doom,
    With smiles of innocence and unambitious play,
    Passed the rapid hours away :
The royal children of my heart and home,
Niall, the heir of hundred-battled Con,
And Corc, of Eogan-More, the not less glorious son.[34]

As Ferguson says later, who would suppose that two
lines so primitive and curt as

My two foster-children were not slack,
Niall of Tara, and Corc of pleasant Cashel

could be 'Pindaricised into such a soaring Olympic?'
(IV, 453).

Charlotte Brooke and the Hardiman translators imposed on their Irish originals the metrical patterns and conventional language of the English poetry of their time. It was this tendency, this inclination to imitate the contemporary and worn-out fashions of English verse, that was their chief drawback as translators of Irish poetry. For despite their realisation of the need to preserve the spirit of the poems they were translating, and the repeated assertions of their attempts to do so, they cloaked the simple, homely thoughts of the originals in an effete, balanced eighteenth-century language, and fitted the alien metrical patterns of the Irish to tight and inflexible English metres.

Charlotte Brooke had been conditioned to accept the eighteenth-century habits of verse as the only correct ones: she chooses, therefore, rhyming couplets for some of her translations and gives others the form of classical odes, with strophe and anti-strophe, and such alien artificialities. She recognises distinctive qualities in the originals, but she is incapable of finding a technique to transfer these qualities into English poetry. She speaks, for example, of the power of the Irish language in presenting 'beautiful and affecting' simplicity on the one hand, and heroic grandeur on the other. The eighteenth century was unattuned to either sublime simplicity or heroic grandeur. Charlotte Brooke's failing, therefore, was not a personal failing, but a failing of the age. She was attempting, without having discovered a technique for doing so, to present heroic and essentially pastoral poetry in a mock-heroic and mock-pastoral age. The manner of the eighteenth century lingered on, especially in the hands of minor practitioners of verse. The less individual a writer is, the more he is inclined to follow, as the Hardiman translators were inclined to follow, the neutral stereotyped style of a previous age.

The failure of Charlotte Brooke and the Hardiman translators was partly a matter of technique, partly a matter of knowledge. The customs, manners of society, and techniques of poetry that lay behind the Irish originals were unknown to an English civilisation. In the case of 'Gracey Nugent', for example, it was a natural undertaking for the author, Carolan, to celebrate his patroness. He was merely discharging a duty, whereas in the English world of the eighteenth century, such a verse celebration would be an artificial undertaking, especially if the patron were a woman. Misinterpreting the occasion of the poem, Charlotte Brooke and the Hardiman translators misinterpreted the tone, believing it to be that of a love-sick swain celebrating his lady, with the language and metre that such a situation implied. Immersed as they were in the effete eighteenth-century poetic practices of their day, ignorant of the social manners that produced the Irish poems, and over-defensive of poetry they were presenting to the public for the first time, Charlotte Brooke and the Hardiman translators were incapable of finding a natural style for their translations.

A translator could only begin to succeed when he had immersed himself imaginatively in the civilisation that produced the Irish poems, and that is why Ferguson struggles to understand the heart of Irish society before the introduction of English manners. This, however, was only the beginning. A translator had to be capable of the bold step of deciding that since it was impossible to reproduce in English verse the exact effects of Irish verse it would be better to render the poem in a literal English as close as possible to the Irish. This is Ferguson's starting-point. James Hardiman and Charlotte Brooke felt that a literal translation did the Irish bard a poetic injustice. For Ferguson, however, it is only 'by adhering to the strict severity of literal translation' (IV, 154) that the content of the original could be preserved unmutilated, even though idiomatic differences between the two languages produced in the translation 'an uncouth and difficult hesitation' (III, 460). Ferguson had not realised that this same uncouthness and hesitation would become before the end of the century, in the hands of Douglas Hyde, a grace, a way in which the freshness and distinctive style of the original could be communicated into the translated poem. But he was on the right track. He considered these poems as 'indexes of the tone and taste of native Irish society', as keys to the 'humours and genius' of the Catholic Irish.[35] That genius and society had to be thoroughly understood before the second, more difficult task could be attempted, that of creating an English poem that was comparable to the Irish poem.

A successful translator must not only penetrate imaginatively the civilisation that produced the literature he is translating, but he must also penetrate the imaginative possibilities of the language of the originals. There is no evidence to suggest that some of the

Hardiman translators even knew the Irish language: Furlong is on record as endeavouring to express himself in his translations as 'he conceived the bard would have done, had he composed in English.'[36] Ferguson's literal translations, on the other hand, demonstrate his total command over the Irish language, his thorough understanding of its nuances of sound and its technical and poetic possibilities. The literal translations reproduce exactly the content and tone of the originals, and some of the idioms. In the first stanza of his translation of 'Roisin Dubh', for example, he is prepared to do violence to the English language to render the Irish idiom, 'ná biodh brón ort':

> Oh rose bud, let there not be sorrow on you on account
> of what happened you :
> The friars are coming over the sea, and they are moving
> on the ocean :
> Your pardon will come from the pope and from Rome
> in the East,
> And spare not the Spanish wine on my Roiseen dubh.
>
> (IV, 157)

Or note the idioms in his brilliant translation of 'The County Mayo', prepared with his friend George Fox:[37]

> The Irrul girls are altered — 'tis proud they're grown
> and high,
> With their hair-bags and their top knots — for I pass
> their buckles by —
>
> (III, 466)

Yeats seems to remember the idiom ('They have schooling of their own, but I pass their schooling by') in a late poem, 'The Curse of Cromwell', in which he also reproduces a quotation from the eighteenth-century poet Aodhagan O Rathaille: 'His fathers served their fathers before Christ was crucified.'

In his finished verse translations, Ferguson introduces into English some of the metrical structures that are distinctive to Irish poetry, without losing the texture and tone of the originals in a mere mechanical reproduction of metrical peculiarities. The disciplined form, the strict and athletic movement that he gave his translations of early bardic remains, he replaced in his versions of seventeenth and eighteenth-century love poems by a more flexible line of varying tempo, the long lingering line with its halting unemphatic rhythm.

Technical brilliance, however, is only a preliminary to true translation. In translation, the violet, as Shelley says, must spring again from the root.[38] A flower, a different flower, a different poem perhaps, is created, but from the same root of emotion and expression. A literal translation may capture the sense, tone, and idiom of the original. *But it is not a poem.* The translator must be a poet and must be so moved by the emotion and situation that led to the creation of the original poem that he creates in another language a poem comparable to the original. When Ferguson is not moved by the situation of the poem, as by the formal panegyrics of Carolan for example, his verse translations are stiff and formal. Even when his heart is moved, as is clearly the case in his literal translation of 'Uileacan Dubh O' quoted above, his verse translation can be stultified and stilted. But usually when his heart is moved by the emotion of

61

the original, and when he is able to preserve its metrical distinctiveness, as in 'Cashel of Munster', 'Cean Dubh Deelish', 'Pastheen Finn', and 'The Fair Hills of Ireland', he produces poems that are startling and strange, a type of poem that, with one exception, had been unknown in the history of Anglo-Irish verse.

In creating his poems in English from the Irish originals Ferguson experienced a number of difficulties. One difficulty related to language: idiom and vocabulary. Regarding idiom, Ferguson counsels, the translator must avoid grotesqueness on the one hand and colloquial tameness on the other, the 'happy mean' lying 'much nearer the extreme of quaintness than that of the commonplace' (IV, 529). Ferguson turns from the effete commonplace language the Hardiman translators had used, chooses quaintness for his own translations, and opens the way in which Douglas Hyde later successfully tackled the problem of rendering Irish idiom in the English language. Regarding vocabulary, he advises that the 'classic language' of Pope must be avoided as well as the 'slang' of Donnybrook. He chooses a simple diction which was well suited to the homely thoughts of the originals. A more difficult problem was the power of the Irish language to compress meaning and yet repeat the same thought in a variety of ways, making it almost impossible for the translator to preserve the measure of the original poem:

> The main difficulty, and one which is in some cases insurmountable, consists in the multitude of words in the original forming a measure which frequently does not afford room for more than half the English ex-

pressions requisite for their adequate translation. This arises from the ellipsis of aspirated consonants and concurrent vowels, which frequently slurs three or four words into a single dactyl, and compresses the meaning into so small bounds, that the translator is driven either to lengthen the measure, and thus make his version incompatible with the tune of the original, if a song, and indeed with its spirit and character in any case, or else to double each stanza, and by a dilation as prejudicial to the genius of his subject as the over compression of too strict adherence, to lose the raciness of translation in the effete expansion of a paraphrase.

(IV, 529)

A related difficulty was the apparent incongruity in English between the intricate air of the original and the simplicity of the language and emotions expressed, the reconciliation between measure and sentiment:

We do not here allude to the compressed character of Irish versification before noticed; but to the marked difference between the characters of the prosody and the sentiment, rendered still more striking where the original is associated with any of the more ancient melodies. Here, while the rhythm and music breathe the most plaintive and pathetic sentiment, the accompanying words, in whatever English dress they may be invested, present a contrast of low and ludicrous images as well as of an incondite simplicity of construction the most striking and apparently absurd. (IV, 529)

Ferguson is not always able to overcome these technical difficulties in his English translations. The original of 'The Coolun', for example, combines technical brilliance with an extraordinary simplicity and directness. The last stanza is utterly stark and simple, yet elaborately melodious:

63

An cuimhin leat-sa an oídhche bhídh tu-sa agus me-si,
Fá bhun an chrainn chaorthainn a's an oídhche ag cur
    chuisneadh,
Ní raibh foscath ó'n ngaoíth aguinn ná dídeán ó'n
    bh-fearthainn,
Acht mo chóta chur fúinn agus do gúna chur tharainn.[39]

Rendered literally the stanza reads:

Do you remember that night when you and I were
Under the ash tree and the night freezing,
We had no shelter from the wind or refuge from the
    rain,
But my coat under us and your dress over us.

The intricate rhythm of the music combined with the
stark simplicity of the language makes this stanza
almost untranslatable in an English which preserves
the technical intricacy and the simple thought. Ferguson retains in his verse translation the exact number
of syllables required for the air, but to do this he
elaborates the simple sentiments of the original and
introduces new thoughts and images. In this process
the poignancy, earthiness, and immediacy of the
original are lost, and a poem is produced which is
more reminiscent of an English ballad than of the
Irish original:

Oh, love, do you remember
    When we lay all night alone,
Beneath the ash in the winter storm,
    When the oak wood round did groan?
No shelter then from the blast had we,
    The bitter blast and sleet,
But your gown to wrap about our head,
    And my coat round our feet.

64

In his translation of 'The Coolun', therefore, Ferguson elaborates the thoughts of the original in order to preserve the elaborate air, but elsewhere, in the 'Boatman's Hymn', for example, he sacrifices technical intricacy to retain immediacy. In the Irish original the poet is displaying his technical skill, but no matter how much he parades it, he retains the immediacy of a conversation between a boat and a rock. In an intermediate version Ferguson creates the technical rhythm of the original by imitating its internal rhymes, its assonance and alliteration, even though he has to take some liberties with the thought in order to achieve this:

> Oh Whillan, rough, bold-faced rock, that stoop'st o'er
>   the bay,
> Look forth at the new barque beneath me cleaving her
>   way;
> Saw ye ever, on sea or river, 'mid the mounting of spray,
> Boat made of a tree that urges through the surges like
>   mine to-day,
>   On the tide-top, the tide-top?
>
> "I remember," says Whillan, "a rock I have ever been;
> And constant my watch, each day, o'er the sea-wave
>   green;
> But of all that I ever of barques and of galleys have seen,
> This that urges through the surges beneath you to-day is
>   queen.
>   On the tide-top, the tide-top."
>   (*Lays*, p. 173)

In his final verse version Ferguson omits these 'duplications and crassitudes', simplifies the stanzaic form, while yet retaining some of the assonance and alliteration, in order to capture the movement, buoyancy, and immediacy that is at the heart of the poem:

> Whillan, ahoy! old heart of stone,
> Stooping so black o'er the beach alone,
> Answer me well — on the bursting brine
> Saw you ever a bark like mine?
> > On the tide-top, the tide-top,
> > > Wherry *aroon*, my land and store!
> > On the tide-top, the tide-top,
> > > She is the boat can sail *go leor.*

> Says Whillan, — "Since first I was made of stone,
> I have looked abroad o'er the beach alone —
> But till to-day, on the bursting brine,
> Saw I never a bark like thine,"
> > On the tide-top, the tide-top, &c.

Ferguson's translations of 'Cashel of Munster', 'Cean Dubh Deelish', 'Pastheen Finn', and 'The Fair Hills of Ireland' achieve a brilliant balance between the technical richness of the originals, their simple language, and the immediacy of the emotions expressed. When possible he reproduces their distinctive cadences, basically the trisyllabic metre strengthened with intricate interlacings of vowel and consonantal correspondences, making the rhythm stately, hesitant, unemphatic, and strange, almost at times like the movement of a funeral march.[40] In contrast to English verse, where the voice moves naturally from stress to stress, the stresses in these poems are not so clearly marked, while the unstressed syllables are more fully pronounced. And yet, what makes these poems unique and fresh is, as well as their technical achievement, Ferguson's creation of poems in English that have the same emotional roots as the originals. 'The Fair Hills of Ireland', for example, reproduces the richness of the effects of the original, an exotic romantic portrait of the bounty and beauty of Ireland, created as much by the internal music and delayed rhythm as by the content which the sounds mime. Yet the feeling at the centre of the poem, the poet's emotion for the country he evokes, makes it into much more than a technical feat:

> A plenteous place is Ireland for hospitable cheer,
> > *Uileacan dubh O!*
> Where the wholesome fruit is bursting from the yellow
> barley ear,
> > *Uileacan dubh O!*
> There is honey in the trees where her misty vales
> expand,
> And her forest paths, in summer, are by falling waters
> fann'd,
> There is dew at high noontide there, and springs i' the
> yellow sand,
> > On the fair hills of holy Ireland.

At times Ferguson finds it necessary to take liberties with his originals in order to preserve the immediacy of the emotion or the integrity of the English poem. The Irish originals combine technical brilliance of expression with an extraordinary simplicity and directness of emotion. This combination makes them extremely difficult to translate. The metres are intricate and elaborate, the emotion urgent and passionate, the language direct, concrete, and physical. Like Hebrew poetry, the language of these poems seems at a primitive stage of development, and thought which can only be rendered metaphorically or abstractly in English is expressed in Irish in direct physical terms.

The fourth stanza of 'Pastheen Finn', for example, is expressed with such extraordinary earthiness and physicality that it is almost impossible to translate it literally into another language and still retain its integrity as a poem:

> Bhídh mé naoí n-oídhehe a'm luídhe go bocht,
> O bheith sínte faoí an dílinn idir dhá thor;
> A chomainn mo chroídhe istigh! 's mé ag smuaíneadh
>   ort,
> 'S ná faghainn-si le fead 'ná le glaodh thú.
>   A's óró bog liom-sa ! bog liom-sa ! bog liom-sa !
>   A's óró bog liom-sa ! a chailín dheas, dhonn !
>   A's óró bhogfainn, da m-bogfádh-sa liom,
>   A d-tús an phluide go sásta.[41]

Rendered literally this becomes:

> I was nine nights lying poorly,
> From being stretched under the torrent between two
>   bushes;
> Companion of my heart inside ! and I thinking of you,
> And that I couldn't get you with a whistle or a call !
>   Oro, move with me! move with me! move with me!
>   Oro, move with me! sweet girl, brown!
>   And I would move, if you would move with me,
>   On the top of the blanket contentedly.

The alignment is literally physical in Irish. Also, direct translation of an idiom like 'mo chroídhe istigh', literally 'my heart inside', would be ludicrous in English. Ferguson captures the rhythm of the refrain and through a cunning maze of sound he creates the intricacy and intensity of feeling in the Irish poem. But by introducing a reference to the elements in the third line of the refrain, he perhaps intentionally camouflages the direct sexual overtones of the original, or at least makes them ambiguous, suggesting not the movement of bodies, but the movement of flight and an invitation to exile. Some of the obvious rakish quality of the original is therefore absent from Ferguson's translation. Yet he has so absorbed the emotion at the centre of the poem, the sense of strained longing and expectancy, the feeling of despair in the poet's passionate cry of desire, that he creates a poem that has qualities in English apart from the Irish but which never would have existed but for the Irish original:

> Nine nights I lay in longing and pain,
> Betwixt two bushes, beneath the rain,
> Thinking to see you, love, once again;
> But whistle and call were all in vain!
>> Then, Oro, come with me! come with me! come
>> with me!
>> Oro, come with me! brown girl, sweet!
>> And, oh! I would go through snow and sleet,
>> If you would come with me, brown girl, sweet!

'Cashel of Munster' is a brilliant translation:

> I'd wed you without herds, without money, or rich
> array,
> And I'd wed you on a dewy morning at day-dawn grey;
> My bitter woe it is, love, that we are not far away
> In Cashel town, though the bare deal board were our
> marriage-bed this day!

> Oh, fair maid, remember the green hill side,
> Remember how I hunted about the valleys wide;
> Time now has worn me; my locks are turned to grey,
> The year is scarce and I am poor, but send me not, love,
> away!

Not only does Ferguson reproduce the stately unemphatic rhythms of the original, but in the stanzas quoted he reproduces some of their exact vowel sounds. His literal translation of the first two lines is as follows:

> I would marry you without cattle, without money, and
>   without much portion,
> And I would marry you on a dewy morning at whitening
>   of the day.

(IV, 167)

He alters 'without much portion' to 'rich array' to capture an exact vowel sound of the original while still retaining the sense. More brilliantly, he alters 'whitening of the day' to 'day-dawn grey', thereby introducing a distinctive feature of Irish poetry into English poetry, that of concluding a line of verse with three monosyllabic feet. The first stanza of the original concludes similarly, 'clár bog déal'. Later Yeats uses this technical device to conclude many of his poems: 'deep heart's core', for example, in 'The Lake Isle of Innisfree', or 'With an old foul tune' in 'The States-man's Holiday', or 'And I cried tears down' in 'Crazy Jane on the Mountain'.

Ferguson therefore captures in English the technical intricacy of the Irish poem, giving his own poem a strange haunting quality and rendering it capable of being sung to the elaborate air of the original. More importantly, he grasps the central human situation at the core of the poem, the pressing expression of desire of a poet for his beloved, even though the only bed they could enjoy would be a bare deal board. There is nothing artificial or abstract or idealised in either Ferguson's poem or the original. We have the sense of a real situation and an actual occasion. The Hardiman translator, on the other hand, takes flagrant liberties with the original, omitting 'everything that gives the poem its immediacy, its agonizing freshness — the place-name, the deal board, the marriage-bed.' [42] The translation, like so many of the other translations in the *Irish Minstrelsy*, presents a flux of outworn platitudes and words, a surfeit of clichéd sentimental expression, presented in English metrical forms that had long been sapped of vitality or vigour:

> I would wed you my dear girl without herds or land,
> Let me claim as a portion but thy own white hand;
> On each soft dewy morning shall I bless thy charms,
> And clasp thee all fondly in my anxious arms.
>
> It grieves me, my fairest, still here to stay,
> To the south, to the south love! let us haste away;
> There plainly, but fondly, shall thy couch be spread,
> And this breast be as a pillow to support thy head.[43]

The Hardiman translators were reluctant to retain the earthy images of the originals. The translator D'Alton, for example, blushing to think of the figure Pastheen Finn would make in the poet's embrace between 'two barrels of porter' staved off the ignominy in an egregiously evasive translation:

> With what rapture I'd quaff it, were I in the hall
> Where feasting — and pledging — and music recall
> Proud days of my country! while she on my breast
> Would recline, my heart's twin one! and hallow the feast.[44]

The Hardiman translation of 'Cean Dubh Deelish' bears no relation to the original:

Oh ! sweetest and dearest of maidens behold me,
　All lowly before thee thy victim must fall;
Oh ! let thy white arms in fondness enfold me,
　Oh ! let thy lov'd lips my lost spirit recall.
There are maidens around that too partially view me,
　Aye, girl, whose gay glances enchant and enthrall;
But idly they watch me, and vainly they woo me,
　For thee *Cean Dubh Deelish* I'd fly from them all.

Then dearest and sweetest come let me caress thee,
　Come lay thy lov'd cheek on the breast of thy slave;
Where is he who could see and not seek to possess thee,
　Oh ! such must be heartless and cold as the grave.[45]

Ferguson's translation, on the other hand, with the
exception of one line (the exclusion of 'smooth white
hand' which he perhaps felt would diffuse the immediacy of desire he was attempting to create) is
extraordinarily close to the original and yet elaborately mellifluous :

Put your head, darling, darling, darling,
　Your darling black head my heart above;
Oh, mouth of honey, with the thyme for fragrance,
　Who, with heart in breast, could deny you love?
Oh, many and many a young girl for me is pining,
　Letting her locks of gold to the cold wind free,
For me, the foremost of our gay young fellows;
　But I'd leave a hundred, pure love, for thee !
Then put your head, darling, darling, darling,
　Your darling black head my heart above;
Oh, mouth of honey, with the thyme for fragrance,
　Who, with heart in breast, could deny you love?

Ferguson reproduces boldly in English a primitive
device of emphasis in the original, repetition, and
strengthens it in the second line by a device of paral-
lelism, that is repeating the same words in a slightly

different form. Charlotte Brooke took this feature of the Irish language as something impossible to overcome in translation, but here Ferguson has transformed what could in lesser hands be a weakness into a strength. Ferguson's poem captures the innocent physicality, the series of passionate cries, the urgency of sensuous desire that constitutes the original. And yet, no matter how urgent his English poem is, no matter how direct an outpouring of emotion it seems, it is less direct and less urgent than the Irish poem, where the poet, expressing his emotion in concrete physical terms, does not even consider it necessary to mention 'heart' in the line 'Your darling black head my heart above'. Inversion in English usually suggests strain, but the inversion here communicates strangeness and immediacy. Douglas Hyde translates the lines literally :

> Black Head, Darling, Darling, Darling,
> Black Head, Darling, move over to me.[46]

Although Hyde is faithful to the letter of the Irish poem, in doing so he sacrifices the effects Ferguson achieves in penetrating to the heart of the emotion and in producing a poem that is in a different language the equivalent of an Irish original.

In his more inspired translations Ferguson has so assimilated the technical manner, emotions, and situation at the heart of the originals that he produces poems that are not antiquarian oddities or academic exercises but startlingly direct, fresh, and original. Indeed it was not until these translations were made, and those of his independent forerunner, Jeremiah

Callanan, that, in Yeats's words, anything of 'an honest style' came into Anglo-Irish poetry.[47] Ferguson's translations show a marked self-confidence and strength of mind, a genius of originality as he broke boldly with the established mode of Anglo-Irish translation and furnished later translators with a model in which simplicity had not been sacrificed to false sophistication nor truth to convention. It is true that Callanan had attempted in a few of his translations, 'The Outlaw of Loch Lene' for example, 'a union of Gaelic thought, rhythm, and vowel pattern',[48] and had used the distinctive undulating line that Ferguson and other translators were to use. But Ferguson's pioneering position in this area of Anglo-Irish literature has never been realised. His translations from the Irish were published in the *Dublin University Magazine* in 1834, but were not collected until 1865 in *The Lays of the Western Gael*. Literary historians, consequently, have concluded that Ferguson was influenced by James Clarence Mangan and Edward Walsh rather than the opposite way around.[49] Edward Walsh indirectly declares his indebtedness to Ferguson in the outline of his approach to the translation of Irish poetry in his *Irish Popular Songs* in 1847. Also, some of Mangan's finer translations were directly inspired by Ferguson's. 'O'Hussey's Ode to the Maguire' was based on Ferguson's literal version which Mangan 'greatly admired . . . and wished to make better known'.[50] Similarly, 'Dark Rosaleen',[51] 'The Boatman's Hymn',[52] and 'Lament over the Ruins of Teach Molaga'[53] were based on the literal translations Ferguson had published in 1834. Unlike Ferguson, Man-

74

gan knew little Irish, and in the creation of his English poems he took considerable liberties with the Irish originals. Ferguson's 'Roisin Dubh', for example, which follows the original very closely, is a love poem, and he makes a convincing case in his commentary that it is the cry of a clerical lover awaiting release from his vow of celibacy rather than a political allegory:

> The course is long over which I brought you from
>   yesterday to this day —
> Over mountains I went with her, and under sails across
>   the sea:
> The Erne I passed at a bound, though great the flood,
> And there was music of strings on each side of me and
>   my Roiseen dubh. . . .
>
> If I had a plough I would plough against the hills;
> And I would make the gospel in the middle of the mass
>   for my black rose-bud:
> I would give a kiss to the young girl that would give her
>   youth to me,
> And I would make delights behind the fort with my
>   Roiseen dubh.
>
> The Erne shall be in its strong flood — the hills shall be
>   uptorn;
> And the sea shall have its waves red, and blood shall be
>   spilled;
> Every mountain-valley, and every moor throughout
>   Ireland shall be on high,
> Some day before (you) shall perish, my Roiseen dubh.
>
> (IV, 157-8)

It must be remembered that Ferguson's is a literal translation, but Mangan, with a number of consummate imaginative strokes, transforms what is essentially a love poem into a poem symbolic of the aspirations of a repressed nation:

75

Over hills and through dales
    Have I roamed for your sake;
All yesterday I sailed with sails
    On river and on lake.
The Erne, at its highest flood,
    I dashed across unseen,
For there was lightning in my blood,
    My Dark Rosaleen !
    My own Rosaleen !
O ! there was lightning in my blood,
Red lightning lightened through my blood,
    My Dark Rosaleen ! . . .

I could scale the blue air,
    I could plough the high hills,
O, I could kneel all night in prayer,
    To heal your many ills !
And one beaming smile from you
    Would float like light between
My toils and me, my own, my true,
    My Dark Rosaleen !
    My fond Rosaleen !
Would give me life and soul anew,
A second life, a soul anew,
    My Dark Rosaleen !

O ! the Erne shall run red
    With redundance of blood,
The earth shall rock beneath our tread,
    And flames wrap hill and wood,
And gun-peal, and slogan cry,
    Wake many a glen serene,
Ere you shall fade, ere you shall die,
    My Dark Rosaleen !
    My own Rosaleen !
The Judgement Hour must first be nigh,
Ere you can fade, ere you can die,
    My Dark Rosaleen ! [54]

76

The transference of passionate feeling from the beloved to the poet's country was a natural one for Mangan to make. There had been a whole tradition of poetry in the Irish language, the *aisling*, in which this transference was made, and one of Mangan's own original poems, 'A Vision of Connaught in the Thirteenth Century', is in this tradition. The identification of beloved and country is implicit in the love poems we have been analysing, for hanging over the passionate expression of love is the terrible threat of a deprivation, both personal and national, that can never be alleviated. The clerical lover can never be released from his vow of celibacy; the lover in 'Cashel of Munster' can never have anything more than a bare deal board to offer as a bed for his beloved. Individual sensation or the expectation of sensual fulfilment almost withers up in the non-licentious expression of feelings that can never be gratified while the state of the nation continues. Also, the stately, hesitant rhythms of the originals and Ferguson's translations suggest at times something of the movement of a formal funeral march. Thus we have the irony of a passionate love poem being expressed in a rhythm appropriate for an elaborate lamentation, a rhythm that evokes the deprivation that hangs like a heavy cloud over the nation and the lovers.

A distinctive Anglo-Irish literature was not possible until there had been some meeting-point between the two cultures that make up the Irish nation. Ferguson's analysis of the qualities of Irish poetry in 1834 and his assessment of the character of the people who produced this poetry was the first time an enlightened member of the ascendant nation with original literary sensitivities had investigated imaginatively the cultural heritage of his Catholic countrymen. Out of that investigation came the consciousness of a distinctive literary tradition and the introduction into Anglo-Irish poetry of a distinctive style. Indeed, so significant were Ferguson's translations from the Irish that we can point with conviction to 1834 as marking the beginning of the movement that produced a distinctive Irish literature in English.

It is well to remember Ferguson's achievement as a translator of Irish poetry, but equally important to realise that if his literary exertions had been confined solely to this field of Anglo-Irish literature he would be a far less significant figure in nineteenth-century Ireland than he is. Ferguson was not interested in translation as a pastime, nor even as an art. He was filled with the broader desire of laying the foundations of a national literature. When he had completed his translations of Irish poems, therefore, he turned to Irish legend and history and began his poetic presentations in English of the legends which ultimately became the chief source of inspiration for Irish writers. Ferguson dedicated fifty years of versatile literary activity in making these legends the subject matter of a new and distinctive literature. It is interesting, though, that his starting-point was exactly the same as that of his Protestant compatriots over half a century later: Yeats, Hyde, Lady Gregory, and Synge. Like Ferguson, their search at the beginning of their literary careers was for the traditions that lay buried in peasants' huts and cottages, the folklore, poetry and myths that provided them with the materials for a distinctive national literature, and through which they too achieved an ascendancy of the heart.

NOTES ON THE TEXT

1 Robert Louis Stevenson and Lloyd Osbourne, *The Wrecker* (New York 1906), p. 480.

2 *The Lighter Side of Irish Life* (London and Edinburgh 1911), p. 16.

3 National Library of Scotland, MS. 4131, fol. 34, Ferguson to John Blackwood (16 August 1858); and MS. 4046, fol. 158, Ferguson to Robert Blackwood (9 April 1838).

4 See Rosamund Jacob, *The Rise of the United Irishmen* (London 1937), p. 72. For a good evocation of the literary and social background of the Belfast of the time, see Brendán O Buachalla, *I mBéal Feirste cois cuain* (Dublin 1968).

5 Address of William Drennan at the Opening of the Institution, in Joseph Fisher and John Robb, *Royal Belfast Academical Institution Centenary Volume 1810-1910* (Belfast 1913), p. 205.

6 *Dublin University Magazine*, II (November 1833), 589-90. Since I shall be quoting extensively and frequently from Ferguson's articles in the *Dublin University Magazine*, the appropriate volume and page number shall be cited, when appropriate, in the text.

7 *Blackwood's Edinburgh Magazine*, XXXIII (January 1833), 88.

8 Fisher and Robb, *Royal Belfast Academical Institution*, p. 106.

9 Mary Catherine Ferguson, *Sir Samuel Ferguson in the Ireland of his Day*, 2 vols. (Edinburgh and London 1896), I, 36. In subsequent references this work will be abbreviated to *Life*.

10 National Library of Scotland, MS. 4035, fol. 211. Ferguson to William Blackwood (21 May 1833).

11 *Life*, I, 42.

12 The first critical edition of Carolan's poems was produced by Tomás O Máille in 1916, as Vol. XVII of the *Irish Texts Society*. See also Donal O'Sullivan, *Carolan : The Life, Times and Music of an Irish Harper*, 2 vols. (London 1958).

13 *The Lays of the Western Gael* (London 1865), pp. 169-70. Unless otherwise specified, all quotations from Ferguson's translations from the Irish are taken from this volume; the exact references shall be cited when appropriate and necessary in the text.

14 I have been unable to locate the sources of 'The Lapful of Nuts', 'Hopeless Love', and 'Mary's Waking'. Indeed, although 'Hopeless Love' and 'Mary's Waking' were included in 'Versions from the Irish' in the *Lays*, it is not at all certain that they are translations at all. Both seem to be original lyrics addressed to Ferguson's much-loved cousin Hessy Gunning (see *Life*, I, 28-30). An early draft of 'Mary's Waking' was called 'Laura', the literary name by which Ferguson addressed his cousin. Certainly the poem has more artifice than the other translations and more restraint and resignation than the other love poems.

15 Brian Inglis, *Roger Casement*. Quoted in *The Irish Times* (12 May 1973).

16 Introduction to James Hardiman's *Irish Minstrelsy* (Shannon 1971), I, vi.

17 Royal Irish Academy, MS. 12N20, 92. Ferguson to Hardiman (28 August 1843).

18 *Irish Minstrelsy*, 2 vols. (London 1831), p. xxxix.

19 *Addenda to the Calendar of the State Papers Relating to Ireland, 1601-3*, ed. R. P. Mahaffy (London 1912), pp. 681-2.

20 'Irish Hospitality, Love, and Poetry', *Gentleman's Magazine*, XXI (October 1751), 467.

21 *European Magazine, and London Review*, II (London 1782), 100.

22 Russell Alspach, *Irish Poetry from the English Invasion to 1798* (London 1943), p. 112.

23 Introduction to *A Book of Irish Verse* (London 1895), p. xiii.

24 Kenneth Heaslip, 'Irish Gaelic Literature (verse) in translation', p. 28. Unpublished B.Litt. dissertation, Trinity College Dublin, 1959.

25 *Reliques of Irish Poetry* (Dublin 1789), p.v.
26 *Ibid.*, p. vii.
27 *Ibid.*, p. vi.
28 *Ibid.*, p. 230.
29 Hardiman, *Irish Minstrelsy*, I, lxxvii - lxxviii.
30 *Ibid.*, I, lxxviii.
31 *Reliques*, pp. v-vi.
32 *Ibid.*, p. 247.
33 Hardiman, *Irish Minstrelsy*, I, 57.
34 *Ibid.*, II, 183.
35 *Lays*, p. 171.
36 Hardiman, *Irish Minstrelsy*, I, lxxviii.
37 This translation appeared in Ferguson's articles on Hardiman, but in an unpublished letter in 1845 he informed Charles Gavan Duffy that Fox had a greater hand in translating it than he himself : ' "The County Mayo" is not mine, save a few lines. It is by George Fox my friend and co-student in former days' (National Library of Ireland, MS. 5756, fol. 465. Ferguson to Duffy, 1 August 1845).
38 *A Defence of Poetry.*
39 Hardiman, *Irish Minstrelsy*, I, 252. I have transcribed the poem as it appears in Hardiman, but it is clear from the grammatical errors that appear here, and elsewhere, that Hardiman did not take meticulous care with the text of his poems.
40 For an excellent analysis of the technical features of Anglo-Irish poetry see Sean Lucy, 'What is Anglo-Irish Poetry?' in *Irish Poets in English*, ed. Sean Lucy (Cork 1973), pp. 22 ff.
41 Hardiman, *Irish Minstrelsy*, I, 218.
42 Eiléan Ní Chuilleanáin, 'Gaelic Ireland Rediscovered : Courtly and Country Poetry', in *Irish Poets in English*, p. 53.
43 Hardiman, *Irish Minstrelsy*, I, 239.
44 *Ibid.*, I, 219.
45 *Ibid.*, I, 263.
46 *Poems from the Irish*, ed. Monk Gibbon (Dublin 1963), p. 35.

47 *A Book of Irish Verse*, p. xiii.
48 B. G. MacCarthy, 'Jeremiah J. Callanan : His Poetry', *Studies*, XXXV (Dublin, September 1946), 394.
49 Typical of this attitude is a bald statement in *Irish Poets in English* that Ferguson 'did not turn to Irish themes until 1865' (p. 88).
50 D. J. O'Donoghue, *The Life and Writings of James Clarence Mangan* (Edinburgh 1897), p. 122.
51 *Ibid.*, pp. 179-80.
52 Mangan admits this in his 'Anthologia Hibernica', *Dublin University Magazine*, XXIX (February 1847), 241.
53 *Poems of James Clarence Mangan*, ed. D. J. O'Donoghue (Dublin 1903), p. 325.
54 *Ibid.*, pp. 3-5.